At Sylvan, we believe reading is one of life's most important and enriching abilities, and we're glad you've chosen our resources to help your child build this critically important skill. We know that the time you spend with your child reinforcing the lessons learned in school will contribute to his or her love of reading. This love of reading will translate into academic achievement. Successful readers are ready for the world around them; they are prepared to do research, to experience literature, and to make the connections necessary to achieve in school and life.

In teaching reading at Sylvan, we use a research-based, step-by-step process, which includes thought-provoking reading selections and activities. Our Sylvan workbooks are designed to help you to help your child build the skills and confidence that will contribute to his or her success in school.

Included with your purchase of this workbook is a coupon for a discount at a participating Sylvan center. We hope you will use this coupon to further your child's academic journey. Let us partner with you to support the development of a confident, well prepared, independent learner.

The Sylvan Team

Sylvan Learning Center
Unleash your child's potential here

No matter how big or small the academic challenge, every child has the ability to learn. But sometimes children need help making it happen. Sylvan believes every child has the potential to do great things. And, we know better than anyone else how to tap into that academic potential so that a child's future really is full of possibilities. Sylvan Learning Center is the place where your child can build and master the learning skills needed to succeed and unlock the potential you know is there.

The proven, personalized approach of our in-center programs delivers unparalleled results that other supplemental education services simply can't match. Your child's achievements will be seen not only in test scores and report cards but outside the classroom as well. And when your child starts achieving his or her full potential, everyone will know it. You will see a new level of confidence come through in all of your child's activities and interactions.

How can Sylvan's personalized in-center approach help your child unleash the potential you know is there?

• Starting with our exclusive Sylvan Skills Assessment®, we pinpoint your child's exact academic needs.

• Then we develop a customized learning plan designed to meet your child's academic goals.

• Through our method of skill mastery, your child will not only learn and master every skill in a personalized plan, but he or she will be truly motivated and inspired to achieve.

To get started, included with this Sylvan product purchase is $10 off our exclusive Sylvan Skills Assessment®. Simply use this coupon and contact your local Sylvan Learning Center to set up your appointment.

To learn more about Sylvan and our innovative in-center programs, call 1-800-EDUCATE or visit www.SylvanLearning.com. *With over 900 locations in North America, there is a Sylvan Learning Center near you!*

1st Grade
Success with Sight Words

Published in the United States by Random House, Inc., New York, and in Canada by Random House of Canada Limited, Toronto.

www.tutoring.sylvanlearning.com

Created by Smarterville Productions LLC
Producer & Editorial Direction: The Linguistic Edge
Producer: TJ Trochlil McGreevy
Writer: Christina Wilsdon
Cover and Interior Illustrations: Shawn Finley, Tim Goldman, and Duendes del Sur
Layout and Art Direction: SunDried Penguin

First Edition

ISBN: 978-0-307-47932-7
ISSN: 2156-6283

This book is available at special discounts for bulk purchases for sales promotions or premiums. For more information, write to Special Markets/Premium Sales, 1745 Broadway, MD 6-2, New York, New York 10019 or e-mail specialmarkets@randomhouse.com.

PRINTED IN CHINA

10 9 8 7 6 5 4 3 2

Contents

Duck Tracy

Duck Tracy has found some clues. But he needs help! TRACE the words so he can read them.

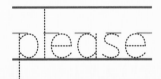

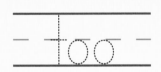

Word Blocks

SAY the words. FILL IN each word block with a word of the same shape.

our	his	her	please

1. h e r

2.

3.

4.

Choosy Suzie

Help Choosy Suzie pick the right words. LOOK at the first word in each row. CIRCLE the word in the row that matches it.

our	hour	our	oar	out
his	hiss	has	his	is
her	her	here	hire	hair
please	pleas	peas	place	please
too	two	too	to	toe

Blank Out

READ each word. LOOK at each picture. WRITE the word to complete each sentence.
HINT: Each word is used only once.

our	his	her	too

May I come in _____?
₁

We like _____ balloons.
₂

He likes _____ mittens.
₃

She plays with _____ cat.
₄

Jiffy Words

Dear Pen Pal

SAY the words. READ the letter to Ling. FILL IN the missing words.
HINT: Each word is used only once.

our	his	her	please	too

Dear Ling,

We are going on a trip. We will bring _____ (1) dog. My dad will bring _____ (2) boat. My mom will bring _____ (3) kite.

Oh, and we will bring my brother _____ (4)! OK, _____ (5) write back.

Bye!

Maria

Be a Poet

It's time to rhyme! READ the poems. FILL IN the blanks with words that rhyme.

| our | her | please | too |

Will you _____ ₁

pass the peas?

Please come to _____ ₂

house in one hour.

I went to the zoo

and the playground _____ ₃ .

The cat likes _____ ₄ .

She makes him purr.

Pick a Picture

TRACE the words. DRAW a line from each word to its matching picture.

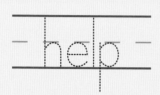

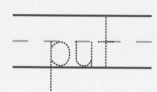

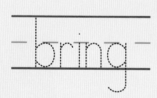

Word Blocks

SAY the words. FILL IN each word block with a word of the same shape.

help	put	take	bring	stop	must

1.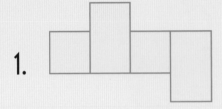

2.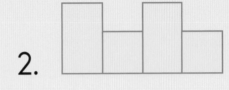

3.

4.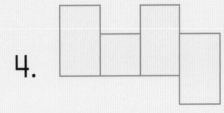

5.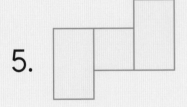

6.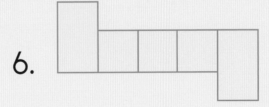

Blank Out

READ each word. LOOK at each picture. WRITE the word to complete each sentence.
HINT: Each word is used only once.

stop	help	must	put

1. I _____ the toy in the box.

2. Quick, _____ that horse!

3. The boy _____ take a bath.

4. Please _____ me chop the log.

Dear Pen Pal

SAY the words. READ the letter to Kia. FILL IN the missing words.
HINT: Each word is used only once.

must	take	put	stop	help	bring

Dear Kia,

Today I had to _____ my dad wash
1

dishes. Then I _____ away my toys. I
2

_____ always feed the cat and _____
3   4

in the mail. I also _____ care of the
5

baby. I can make her _____ crying.
6

What jobs do you do at home?

Your friend, Jamie

Be a Poet

It's time to rhyme! READ the poems. FILL IN the blanks with words that rhyme.

| bring | take | stop | must |

The man _____
1
sweep and dust.

Please _____
2
a piece of cake.

The balloon will pop
if you do not _____!
3

May I _____
4
a song to sing?

Word Hunt

READ the words. CIRCLE the words in the grid. WRITE each word after you circle it. Words go across and down.

help	put	take	stop	must

```
s  t  o  p  m  h
u  a  m  u  s  t
r  k  p  t  a  k
h  e  l  p  s  o
```

_____   _____   _____
- - - - - - -   - - - - - - -   - - - - - - -
_____   _____   _____

          _____   _____
          - - - - - - -   - - - - - - -
          _____   _____

Duck Tracy

Duck Tracy has found some clues. But he needs help! TRACE the words so he can read them.

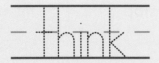

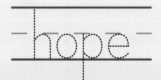

Word Blocks

SAY the words. FILL IN each word block with a word of the same shape.

think   know   wish   hope

1.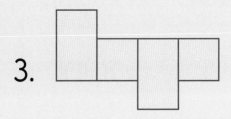

2.

3.

4.

Choosy Suzie

Help Choosy Suzie pick the right words. LOOK at the first word in each row. CIRCLE the word in the row that matches it.

hope	hop	hope	hoop	heap
think	thank	tank	thin	think
wish	wish	wash	was	mash
know	now	no	know	knew

Blank Out

READ each word. LOOK at each picture. WRITE the word to complete each sentence.
HINT: Each word is used only once.

think	know	wish	hope

Make a ___ ___ ___ ___ and blow
out the candles!
₁

I like to sit and ___ ___ ___ ___ ___.
₂

I ___ ___ ___ ___ the rain stops.
₃

Do you ___ ___ ___ ___ how to tie
a shoe?
₄

Criss Cross

READ the clues. FILL IN the right words in the grid.

| her | stop | take | please | hope | wish | put | our |

Across

1. Close your eyes and make a _____!

3. We have a dog. It is _____ pet.

4. The opposite of *go* is _____.

7. Remember to ask nicely and say _____.

Down

2. I _____ you feel better soon.

5. The opposite of *give* is _____.

6. She washed _____ hands.

7. Please _____ your toys in the box.

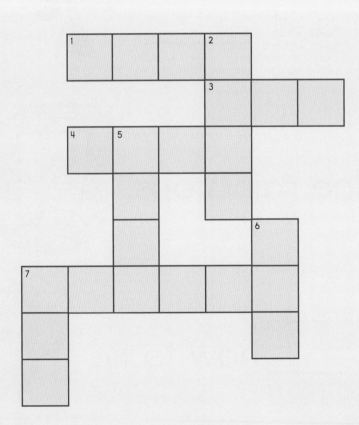

Dear Pen Pal

SAY the words. READ the letter to Nate. FILL IN the missing words.
HINT: Each word is used only once.

bring	too	help	wish	our	hope

Dear Nate,

I am going camping! I will _____ my
1

mom pack _____ bags. We have to
2

_____ our own food and our own
3

dishes _____! I _____ it does not rain.
4   5

I _____ you were coming with us.
6

See you soon!

Ian

On the Farm

Pick a Picture

TRACE the words. DRAW a line from each word to its matching picture.

horse

cow

pig

sheep

duck

chicken

What's This?

LOOK at each animal in the picture. WRITE the word for each animal, using the words on the opposite page.

1

2

3

4

5

6

On the Farm

Name It

LOOK at each picture. READ the words next to the picture. CIRCLE the word that matches the picture.

hose	horse	house
cow	caw	now
big	pug	pig
ship	shop	sheep
chicken	check	chick
deck	dock	duck

I Am a . . .

READ the words. Then READ each sentence. WRITE the word that ends each sentence.

horse	cow	duck	sheep

I say "moo."

I am a _____.
1

I have wool.

I am a _____.
2

I run very fast.

I am a _____.
3

I lay eggs.

I am a _____.
4

On the Farm

Art Starts

READ the story out loud. DRAW a picture for each sentence.

1

"See me fly," said the cow.

2

"See me dance," said the duck.

3

"See me stand on my head," said the pig.

Criss Cross

WRITE the word for each picture clue in the grid.

Blank Out

READ each word. LOOK at each picture. WRITE the word to complete each sentence.
HINT: Each word is used only once.

best	kind	good	funny

This apple tastes very _____!

The _____ cake got a blue ribbon.

Look at the _____ clown.

I am _____ to my cat.

Word Blocks

SAY the words. FILL IN each word block with a word of the same shape.

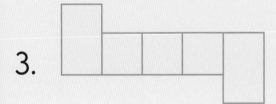

good	better	best	funny

1.

2.

3.

4.

Be a Poet

It's time to rhyme! READ the poems. FILL IN the blanks with words that rhyme.

good	best	better	funny

That big toy bunny

is very _____.

1

A duck feels _____

when the weather is wetter.

I did my _____

on the spelling test!

Soup made of wood?

That is not very _____!

Jot It Down

READ the words. LOOK at each picture. WRITE the word that matches each picture. HINT: Each word is used only once.

better	best	good

This frog made a _____ jump.
1

This frog made a _____ jump.
2

This frog made the _____ jump of all!
3

Duck Tracy

Duck Tracy has found some clues. But he needs help! TRACE the words so he can read them.

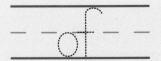

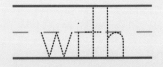

Choosy Suzie

Help Choosy Suzie pick the right words. LOOK at the first
word in each row. CIRCLE the word in the row that matches it.

as	at	has	as	ask
let	lot	let	lit	get
of	off	if	on	of
with	with	will	wit	want
round	sound	ground	round	rind

Word Blocks

SAY the words. FILL IN each word block with a word of the same shape.

as	let	of	with	off	round

1.

2.

3.

4.

5.

6.

Blank Out

READ each word. LOOK at each picture. WRITE the word to complete each sentence.
HINT: Each word is used only once.

round	as	with	off

The dog is _____ tall as the boy.
1

Get _____ the table!
2

He walks _____ his sister.
3

The ball is _____.
4

Dear Pen Pal

SAY the words. READ the letter to Jack. FILL IN the missing words.
HINT: Each word is used only once.

as	let	of	with	off	round

Dear Jack,

I went _____ my dad to the zoo. We saw
1

a giraffe _____ tall as our house, and a
2

turtle as _____ as a plate. Dad _____
3   4

me ride a pony. I was sad to get _____!
5

It was one _____ the best days ever.
6

See you!

Ellie

Word Hunt

READ the words. CIRCLE the words in the grid. WRITE each word after you circle it. Words go across and down.

| as | let | of | with | off | round |

```
r o u n d
i f l o t
o f e a s
w i t h o
```

Duck Tracy

Duck Tracy has found some clues. But he needs help! TRACE the words so he can read them.

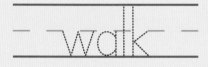

came

going

went

Word Blocks

SAY the words. FILL IN each word block with a word of the same shape.

walk   fly   came   going   went   leave

1.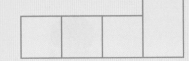

2.

3.

4.

5.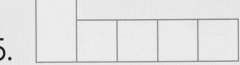

6.

Blank Out

READ each word. LOOK at each picture. WRITE the word to complete each sentence. HINT: Each word is used only once.

| went | going | came | leave |

I am _____ to bed.
1

I will _____ my book here.
2

I _____ to the circus.
3

Look what _____ in the mail!
4

Choosy Suzie

Help Choosy Suzie pick the right words. LOOK at the first
word in each row. CIRCLE the word in the row that matches it.

walk	wake	work	talk	walk
fly	lie	flee	fly	fry
came	come	came	camp	cane
going	going	gong	goat	go
went	want	went	win	what
leave	leaf	loaf	life	leave

Dear Pen Pal

SAY the words. READ the letter to Lucia. FILL IN the missing words.
HINT: Each word is used only once.

walk   fly   came   going   went   leave

Dear Lucia,

I _____ to a slumber party yesterday.
1

I _____ home this morning. I am

_____ to another slumber party tonight!
3

I _____ in about an hour. First I will go
4

for a _____. That will help make the time
5

_____! But boy, am I tired.
6

Bye! Paige

Be a Poet

It's time to rhyme! READ the poems. FILL IN the blanks with words that rhyme.

going	walk	fly	went

The bear _____
1

into the tent.

A plane can _____
2

high up in the sky.

I am _____
3

outside. It's snowing!

I like to talk

to my dog as we _____.
4

Word Hunt

READ the words. CIRCLE the words in the grid. WRITE each word after you circle it.
Words go across and down.

fly   cow   too   walk   round   leave   better   kind   let

```
b e t t e r
c o w t o o
l e a v e u
e f l y t n
t i k i n d
```

Criss Cross

READ the clues. FILL IN the right words in the grid.

best   off   round   kind   with   better   walk

Across

1. Take the dog for a _____ .

2. Good, _____ , best

4. The opposite of *on* is _____ .

5. The opposite of *mean* is _____ .

Down

1. Please come _____ me.

2. Good, better, _____ .

3. A ball is _____ .

Name It

LOOK at each picture. READ the words next to the picture. CIRCLE the word that matches the picture.

bunny   find   funny

wake   walk   wall

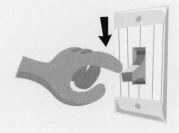

of   oaf   off

duck   deck   dock

lie   flee   fly

Blank Out

READ each word. LOOK at each picture. WRITE the word to complete each sentence.
HINT: Each word is used only once.

kind	with	going	good

The cow is _____ the cat.
1

What _____ of animal is that?
2

He is _____ in the water.
3

Yum! This tastes _____!
4

Put On Your Clothes!

Pick a Picture

TRACE the words. DRAW a line from each word to its matching picture.

shoe

hat

coat

dress

shirt

pants

What's This?

LOOK at the clothes in the picture. WRITE the word for each one, using the words on the opposite page.

Put On Your Clothes!

Jot It Down

LOOK at each picture. READ the words. WRITE the word that matches each picture.
HINT: Each word is used only once.

dress	pants	shirt

The dog has a _____.

1

The ape has a _____.

2

The octopus has _____.

3

I Am a . . .

READ the words. Then READ each sentence. WRITE the word that ends each sentence.

shoe	hat	coat	pants

I go on your legs.

I am _____.
₁

I go on your foot.

I am a _____.
₂

I keep your body warm.

I am a _____.
₃

I go on your head.

I am a _____.
₄

Put On Your Clothes!

Name It

LOOK at each picture. READ the words next to the picture. CIRCLE the word that matches the picture.

show	shoe	shoo
hat	that	hut
cold	cot	coat
dry	dress	press
shirt	short	shut
ants	plants	pants

Art Starts

READ the story out loud. DRAW a picture for each sentence.

1

The dog wore the hat.

2

The dog wore the coat.

3

But he ate the shoe!

Duck Tracy

Duck Tracy has found some clues. But he needs help! TRACE the words so he can read them.

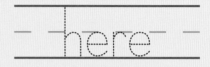

Blank Out

READ each word. LOOK at each picture. WRITE the word to complete each sentence.
HINT: Each word is used only once.

| near | far | here | away |

Go _____, Binky!
1

The moon is _____ away.
2

Come _____, Binky!
3

The duck is _____
4
the water.

Criss Cross

READ the clues. FILL IN the right words in the grid.

away	far	near	here	there

Across

2. The opposite of *here* is _____.

4. The opposite of *far* is _____.

Down

1. The opposite of *near* is _____.

3. The opposite of *there* is _____.

5. Make that bug go _____!

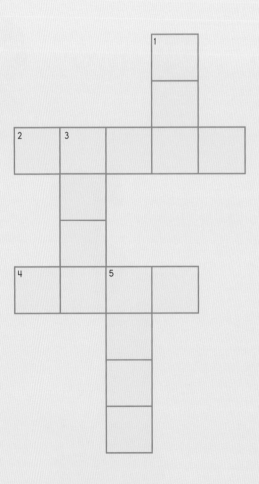

Word Blocks

SAY the words. FILL IN each word block with a word of the same shape.

| away | far | near | here | there |

1.

2.

3.

4.

5.

Duck Tracy

Duck Tracy has found some clues. But he needs help! TRACE the words so he can read them.

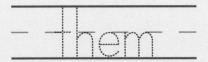

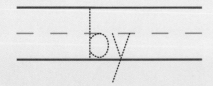

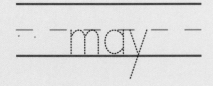

Blank Out

READ each word. LOOK at each picture. WRITE the word to complete each sentence.
HINT: Each word is used only once.

| him | again | by | may |

She gave _____ a puppy.
       1

May I go on the
ride _____?
     2

Mom, _____ I have a cookie?
      3

The cat sat _____ the boy.
            4

Choosy Suzie

Help Choosy Suzie pick the right words. LOOK at the first
word in each row. CIRCLE the word in the row that matches it.

him	hum	him	hen	hem
them	them	thin	time	then
may	my	man	me	may
then	them	then	than	thin
by	buy	bee	by	be
again	gone	age	gain	again

Word Blocks

SAY the words. FILL IN each word block with a word of the same shape.

him	then	again	by	may

1.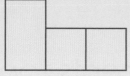

2.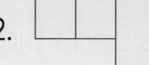

3.

4.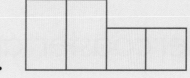

5.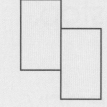

Dear Pen Pal

SAY the words. READ the letter to Jake. FILL IN the missing words.
HINT: Each word is used only once.

him	them	then	again	by	may

Dear Jake,

Today was Ben's birthday. My parents took

_____ to Fun Land. And me too! We rode
  1

the rollercoaster and _____ rode it
                          2

_____! Next my parents drove us _____
  3   4

Shark World. We asked _____ to stop.
                          5

They said we _____ go back someday.
                 6

Bye! Greg

Word Hunt

READ the words. CIRCLE the words in the grid. WRITE each word after you circle it. Words go across and down.

| him | them | then | again | by | may |

```
t h e m h n
h a g a i n
e e b y m a
n t h a r o
```

Blank Out

READ each word. LOOK at each picture. WRITE the word to complete each sentence.
HINT: Each word is used only once.

| them | then | there | pants |

Clean your room, and _____ you may play.
₁

The ape is up _____.
₂

Give me my _____!
₃

She will bring _____ fish.
₄

Be a Poet

It's time to rhyme! READ the poems. FILL IN the blanks with words that rhyme.

there	near	shirt	dress

She can't find her _____
1

because her room is a mess.

Please tell me if _____
2

is a bug in my hair.

Who got dirt

on my favorite _____?
3

Do not go _____
4

the deer!

Duck Tracy

Duck Tracy has found some clues. But he needs help! TRACE the words so he can read them.

 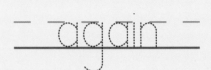

shoe   away   again

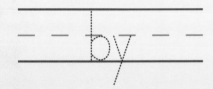

by   far

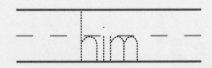

him

Criss Cross

READ the clues. FILL IN the right words in the grid.

| him | coat | horse | there | pants | stop |

Across

1. The opposite of *go* is _____.

4. You can ride a _____.

5. The opposite of *here* is _____.

Down

2. You wear _____ on your legs.

3. You wear a _____ on a cold day.

6. Go to the boy, and give _____ his book.

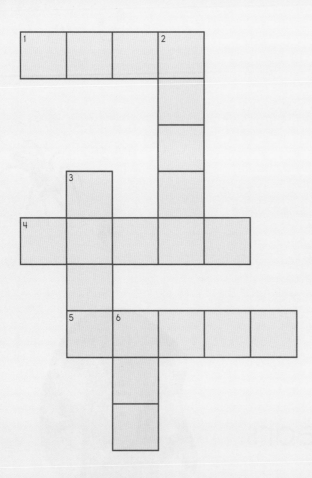

What You Do . . .

Pick a Picture

TRACE the words. DRAW a line from each sentence to its matching picture.

I __eat__ bugs.

I __live__ in a tree.

I __show__ my teeth.

I __hear__ with big ears.

Choosy Suzie

Help Choosy Suzie pick the right words. LOOK at the first
word in each row. CIRCLE the word in the row that matches it.

eat	eat	ate	at	ear
live	love	left	live	leave
show	snow	she	sow	show
hear	ear	hear	heart	hair
tell	tall	tile	tell	tale

What You Do . . .

Blank Out

READ each word. LOOK at each picture. WRITE the word to complete each sentence.
HINT: Each word is used only once.

tell	live	hear	eat

He likes to _____ ice cream.
1

The birds _____ in a tree.
2

Please _____ me a story.
3

I _____ a funny noise.
4

Word Hunt

READ the words. CIRCLE the words in the grid. WRITE each word after you circle it. Words go across and down.

| show | tell | live | hear | eat |

```
s  t  e  l  s
h  e  a  r  h
o  l  t  o  w
w  l  i  v  e
```

What You Do . . .

Art Starts

READ the story out loud. DRAW a picture for each sentence.

1

"I live in a hole," said the mouse.

2

"I eat mice," said the cat.

3

"I hear my mom calling me," said the mouse. "Good-bye!"

Dear Pen Pal

SAY the words. READ the letter to Ty. FILL IN the missing words.
HINT: Each word is used only once.

eat	show	live	tell	hear

Dear Ty,

I have a pet lizard! My dad lets her

_____ in my room. She likes to _____
1   2

worms. I am bringing her to school for

_____ and _____. My friends want
3   4

to _____ all about her.
5

Bye!

Lily

Duck Tracy

Duck Tracy has found some clues. But he needs help! TRACE the words so he can read them.

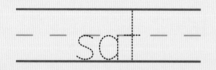

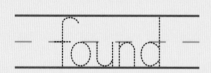

Word Blocks

SAY the words. FILL IN each word block with a word of the same shape.

| ran | ate | sat | had | found |

1.

2.

3.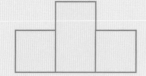

4.

5.

Choosy Suzie

Help Choosy Suzie pick the right words. LOOK at the first
word in each row. CIRCLE the word in the row that matches it.

ran	run	rant	ram	ran
did	dud	deed	did	dad
ate	ate	at	art	ant
sat	sit	sat	set	sad
had	head	hid	hat	had
found	round	fond	found	fund

Blank Out

READ each word. LOOK at each picture. WRITE the word to complete each sentence.
HINT: Each word is used only once.

| sat | ate | found | ran |

The boys _____ fast.
1

We _____ a bug.
2

The girl _____ on the rock.
3

She _____ a hot dog.
4

Dear Pen Pal

SAY the words. READ the letter to Bev. FILL IN the missing words.
HINT: Each word is used only once.

ran	ate	did	found	sat

Dear Bev,

I _____ a weird bug in my house.
1

It _____ my sandwich! I _____
2   3

after it. I used a net, but I still _____
4

not catch it. Then my mom _____ on it.
5

Oops!

Later,

Sid

Jot It Down

LOOK at each picture. READ the words. WRITE the word that matches each picture. HINT: Each word is used only once.

ran	ate	had

The nest _____ two eggs.
₁

The girl _____ the pizza.
₂

The man _____ after the fox.
₃

Word Blocks

SAY the words. FILL IN each word block with a word of the same shape.

birthday   party   name   present   thank   from

1.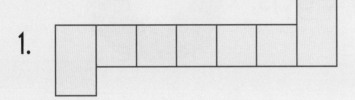

2.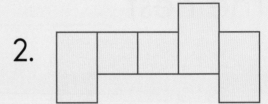

3.

4.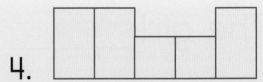

5.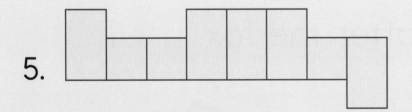

6.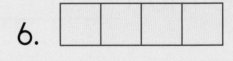

Criss Cross

READ the clues. FILL IN the right words in the grid.

party   present   from   thank   name   birthday

Across

3. You are one year older on your _____.

4. You say "_____ you" when you get a present.

6. This present is _____ Dad.

Down

1. Here is a _____ from Aunt Edna.

2. Please come to my _____.

5. What is your _____?

Blank Out

READ each word. LOOK at each picture. WRITE the word to complete each sentence. HINT: Each word is used only once.

birthday	party	present	name

Thank you for the _____ !
1

Today is my _____ party.
2

Her _____ is Zeena.
3

Sam's birthday _____ was fun.
4

True or False?

LOOK at the picture. READ the sentences. CIRCLE **True** or **False**.

1. The birthday cake is red.   True   False

2. A present is on the table.   True   False

3. The party hats are yellow.   True   False

4. The name on the cake is Pam.   True   False

Art Starts

READ the story out loud. DRAW a picture for each sentence.

1

The birds had a party.

2

They ate a birthday cake.

3

The best present was a
big worm!

Be a Poet

It's time to rhyme! READ the poems. FILL IN the blanks with words that rhyme.

thank	from	party	name

What is the _____
1

of this game?

Can Marty

come to my _____?
2

Please _____
3

your Uncle Hank.

Here is a present _____
4

my sister. It's bubble gum!

Word Hunt

READ the words. CIRCLE the words in the grid. WRITE each word after you circle it. Words go across and down.

hear	ran	found	from	live	show

```
s  f  o  u  n  d
h  e  a  r  a  n
o  f  r  o  m  o
w  l  i  v  e  n
```

_____   _____   _____

_____   _____   _____

Name It

LOOK at each picture. READ the words next to the picture. CIRCLE the word that matches the picture.

	at	eat	end
	hear	hare	here
	rain	rat	ran
	sat	sad	sand
	pantry	pants	party
	found	fond	fund

Dear Pen Pal

SAY the words. READ the letter to Aunt Oona. FILL IN the missing words.
HINT: Each word is used only once.

shirt	party	ate	had	thank	present

Dear Aunt Oona,

I _____ a super birthday! My friends
        1

came to my _____. We _____ cake
            2   3

and ice cream. Oh, _____ you for
                    4

sending me a _____. I like the _____
              5   6

with the cow on it. And the socks too.

Love,

Terry

True or False?

LOOK at the picture. READ the sentences. CIRCLE **True** or **False**.

1. The cat ran after the dog.　　True　False

2. The boy sat on a pig.　　True　False

3. The bird found a worm.　　True　False

4. The squirrel is not in a tree.　　True　False

Duck Tracy

Duck Tracy has found some clues. But he needs help! TRACE the words so he can read them.

Word Blocks

SAY the words. FILL IN each word block with a word of the same shape.

when	where	now	soon	while

1.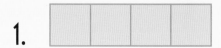

2.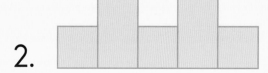

3.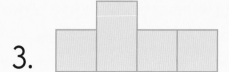

4.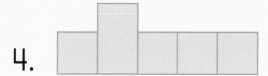

5.

When & Where?

Blank Out

READ each word. LOOK at each picture. WRITE the word to complete each sentence.
HINT: Each word is used only once.

when	where	now	while

You must stop right _____ !

1

I wonder _____ the rain will stop.

2

I like to talk _____ I walk.

3

I do not know _____ my shoe is!

4

Choosy Suzie

Help Choosy Suzie pick the right words. LOOK at the first word in each row. CIRCLE the word in the row that matches it.

when	hen	wet	when	win
where	wear	were	here	where
now	now	new	no	mow
soon	son	soon	moon	sun
while	will	hill	while	wall

Duck Tracy

Duck Tracy has found some clues. But he needs help! TRACE the words so he can read them.

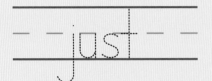

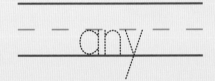

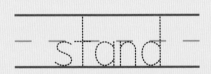

Word Blocks

SAY the words. FILL IN each word block with a word of the same shape.

| could | just | well | any | if | stand |

1.

2.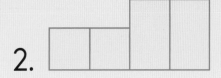

3.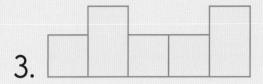

4.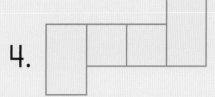

5.

6.

Be a Poet

It's time to rhyme! READ the poems. FILL IN the blanks with words that rhyme.

could	well	stand	any

Just yell

if you do not feel _____ .

1

We can _____

2

and hear the band.

I do not have _____

3

money. Not one penny!

The pig wished he _____

4

build a house out of wood.

Blank Out

READ each word. LOOK at each picture. WRITE the word to complete each sentence.
HINT: Each word is used only once.

just	well	if	stand

He does not feel _____! (1)

She can _____ on her head! (2)

I wonder _____ this bug bites. (3)

The donkey has _____ one box on its back. (4)

Choosy Suzie

Help Choosy Suzie pick the right words. LOOK at the first word in each row. CIRCLE the word in the row that matches it.

could	could	cod	cold	would
just	jest	just	must	jut
well	will	wall	while	well
any	ant	any	tiny	and
if	of	off	lift	if
stand	sand	stand	stone	tan

Dear Pen Pal

SAY the words. READ the letter to Carly. FILL IN the missing words.
HINT: Each word is used only once.

just	any	could	well	if	stand

Dear Carly,

I did not feel _____ (1), so I _____ (2) not

go to the show. I _____ (3) can't _____ (4)

being sick! Mom says _____ (5) I want

to see _____ (6) other show, I can. That

made me feel better!

Your friend,

Elena

Home Sweet Home

Pick a Picture

TRACE the words. DRAW a line from each word to its matching picture.

bed

chair

floor

sofa

table

window

What's This?

LOOK at each item in the picture. WRITE the word for each item, using the words on the opposite page.

1

2

3

4

5

6

Name It

LOOK at each picture. READ the words next to the picture. CIRCLE the word that matches the picture.

	bud	bet	bed
	chair	chore	hair
	four	floor	flour
	sofa	soft	soap
	able	table	tablet
	wind	meadow	window

I Am a . . .

READ the words. Then READ each sentence. WRITE the word that ends each sentence.

window	table	chair	bed

You sleep in me.

I am a _____.
1

You sit on me at the table.

I am a _____.
2

You put dishes on me.

I am a _____.
3

You can see right through me!

I am a _____.
4

Criss Cross

READ the clues. FILL IN the right words in the grid.

| bed | chair | floor | sofa | table |

Across

4. Set the _____ for dinner.

5. Did you mop the _____?

Down

1. Do not tip back in your _____!

2. It is time to go to _____.

3. A _____ is also called a couch.

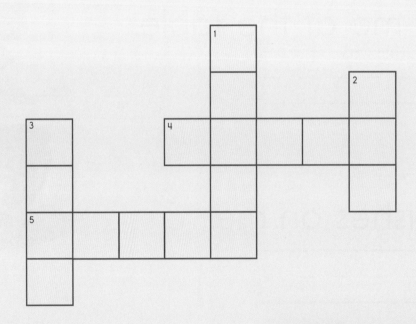

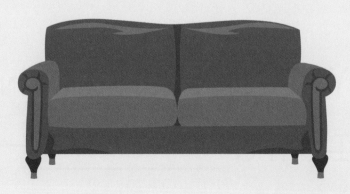

True or False?

LOOK at the picture. READ the sentences. CIRCLE **True** or **False**.

1. There is a seal on the table.   True   False

2. The girl's chair is green.   True   False

3. The floor has spots.   True   False

4. There is a seal under the sofa. True   False

Duck Tracy

Duck Tracy has found some clues. But he needs help! TRACE the words so he can read them.

some

all

every

many

both

much

Word Blocks

SAY the words. FILL IN each word block with a word of the same shape.

some	all	every	many	both	much

1.

2.

3.

4.

5.

6.

Blank Out

READ each word. LOOK at each picture. WRITE the word to complete each sentence.
HINT: Each word is used only once.

all	every	some	both

I have mittens on _____ hands.
1

The sun comes up _____ day.
2

He put _____ of the
3

leaves in one pile.

Would you like _____ pizza?
4

Choosy Suzie

Help Choosy Suzie pick the right words. LOOK at the first word in each row. CIRCLE the word in the row that matches it.

some	sum	some	sun	son
all	all	ball	call	ail
every	even	eave	every	ever
many	money	man	men	many
both	both	booth	bath	birth
much	match	munch	much	muck

Be a Poet

It's time to rhyme! READ the poems. FILL IN the blanks with words that rhyme.

much	all	some	many

Would you like _____
1

bubble gum?

We can _____
2

play with the ball.

You have _____,
3

and I do not have any!

I do not touch _____

our mean cat _____!
4

Dear Pen Pal

SAY the words. READ the letter to Zoey. FILL IN the missing words.
HINT: Each word is used only once.

| some | all | every | many | both | much |

Dear Zoey,

I go riding _____ Saturday. I ride either
1

Star or Joe. I like _____ horses very
2

_____. I have ridden them _____
3   4

times. I wish I could ride _____ the time,
5

but _____ rides are better than none!
6

Bye!

Kelly

Pick a Picture

TRACE the words. DRAW a line from each word to its matching picture.

woman

man

baby

children

friend

Name It

LOOK at each picture. READ the words next to the picture. CIRCLE the word that matches the picture.

worm   woman   woven

men   map   man

baby   bob   bubble

chicken   child   children

fried   friend   frond

I Am a . . .

READ the words. Then READ each sentence. WRITE the word that ends each sentence.

woman   man   baby   friend

I was a girl when I was little.

I am a _____.
1

I am someone who likes you.

I am a _____.
2

I was a boy when I was little.

I am a _____.
3

I am a very young child.

I am a _____.
4

True or False?

LOOK at the picture. READ the sentences. CIRCLE **True** or **False**.

1. The children have blue pails.   True   False

2. A shark is biting the man.   True   False

3. The woman is swimming.   True   False

4. The baby is sleeping.   True   False

Jot It Down

LOOK at each picture. READ the words. WRITE the word that matches each picture.
HINT: Each word is used only once.

man	woman	baby

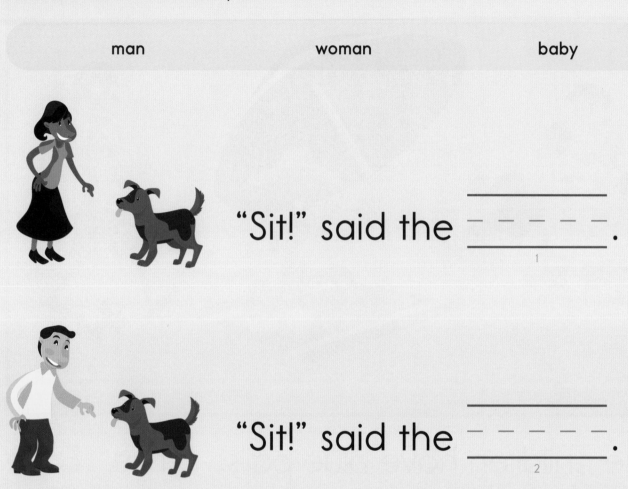

"Sit!" said the _____.
1

"Sit!" said the _____.
2

"Goo-ga-blah!"
said the _____.
3

Art Starts

READ the story out loud. DRAW a picture for each sentence.

1

The children found an egg.

2

A baby dinosaur came out of the egg!

3

"Please be my friend," said the dinosaur.

Word Hunt

READ the words. CIRCLE the words in the grid. WRITE each word after you circle it. Words go across and down.

| where | soon | woman | chair | if | now |

```
n o w o w
s o o n h
c e m l e
c h a i r
t a n f e
```

_____   _____   _____

- - - - -   - - - - -   - - - - -

_____   _____   _____

- - - - -   - - - - -   - - - - -

_____   _____   _____

Dear Pen Pal

SAY the words. READ the letter to Tanya. FILL IN the missing words.
HINT: Each word is used only once.

| now | present | friend | all | baby | tell | duck |

Dear Tanya,

Did I _____ you I have a new
                1

_____ brother? At first he cried
    2

_____ night, but _____ he sleeps.
   3   4

I gave him a _____. It is a little
              5

yellow _____.
         6

Your _____,
      7

Carly

Criss Cross

READ the clues. FILL IN the right words in the grid.

baby　　　table　　　bed　　　woman　　　window　　　sofa

Across

2. A girl grows up to be a _____.

3. You sleep in a _____.

4. A _____ is also called a couch.

Down

1. Please set the _____ for dinner.

2. You look through a _____.

3. A person who was just born is a _____.

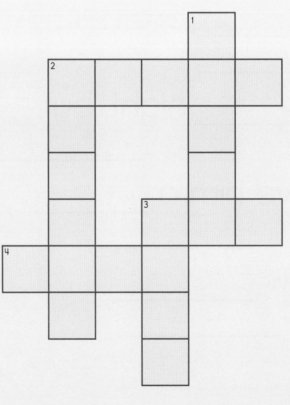

Blank Out

READ each word. LOOK at each picture. WRITE the word to complete each sentence.
HINT: Each word is used only once.

any	much	chair	soon

Will we be there _____?
1

Are there _____
2
cookies in the jar?

He ate so _____ food!
3

The girl sat on the _____.
4

Answers

Page 3
1. her
2. please
3. our
4. his

Page 4

our	hour	(our)	oar	out
his	hiss	has	(his)	is
her	(her)	here	hire	hair
please	pleas	peas	place	(please)
too	two	(too)	to	toe

Page 5
1. too
2. our
3. his
4. her

Page 6
1. our
2. his
3. her
4. too
5. please

Page 7
1. please
2. our
3. too
4. her

Page 8
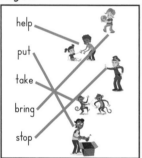

help
put
take
bring
stop

Page 9
1. stop
2. take
3. must
4. help
5. put
6. bring

Page 10
1. put
2. stop
3. must
4. help

Page 11
1. help
2. put
3. must
4. bring
5. take
6. stop

Page 12
1. must
2. take
3. stop
4. bring

Page 13
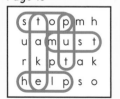

s	t	o	p	m	h
u	a	m	u	s	t
r	k	p	t	a	k
h	e	l	p	s	o

Page 15
1. wish
2. think
3. hope
4. know

Page 16
hope	hop	(hope)	hoop	heap
think	thank	tank	thin	(think)
wish	(wish)	wash	was	mash
know	now	no	(know)	knew

Page 17
1. wish
2. think
3. hope
4. know

Page 18

'w i s h
'o u r
's t o p e
a   h
k   'h
'p l e a s e r
u
t

Page 19
1. help
2. our
3. bring
4. too
5. hope
6. wish

Page 20
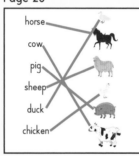

horse
cow
pig
sheep
duck
chicken

Page 21
1. cow
2. chicken
3. pig
4. duck
5. sheep
6. horse

Page 22
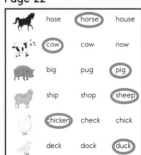

hose	(horse)	house
(cow)	caw	now
big	pug	(pig)
ship	shop	(sheep)
(chicken)	check	chick
deck	dock	(duck)

Page 23
1. cow
2. sheep
3. horse
4. duck

Page 24
Have someone check
your answers.

Page 25
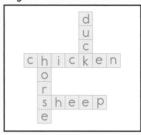

d
u
c
c h i c k e n
h
o
r
s h e e p
e

Page 26
1. good
2. best
3. funny
4. kind

Page 27
1. better
2. best
3. funny
4. good

Page 28
1. funny
2. better
3. best
4. good

Page 29
1. good
2. better
3. best

Page 31
as	at	has	(as)	ask
let	lot	(let)	lit	get
of	off	if	on	(of)
with	(with)	will	wit	want
round	sound	ground	(round)	rind

Page 32
1. with
2. let
3. round
4. off
5. of
6. as

Page 33
1. as
2. off
3. with
4. round

Page 34
1. with
2. as
3. round
4. let
5. off
6. of

Page 35
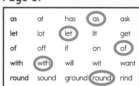

r	o	u	n	d
i	f	l	o	t
o	f	e	a	s
w	i	t	h	o

Page 37
1. went
2. fly
3. walk
4. came
5. leave
6. going

Page 38
1. going
2. leave
3. went
4. came

Page 39
walk	wake	work	talk	(walk)
fly	lie	flee	(fly)	fry
came	come	(came)	camp	cane
going	(going)	gong	goat	go
went	want	(went)	win	what
leave	leaf	loaf	life	(leave)

Page 40
1. went
2. came
3. going
4. leave
5. walk
6. fly

Page 41
1. went
2. fly
3. going
4. walk

Page 42
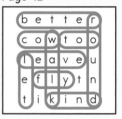

b	e	t	t	e	r
c	o	w	t	o	o
l	e	a	v	e	u
e	f	l	y	t	n
t	i	k	i	n	d

Page 43

w a l k
i
'b e t t e r 'r
e   h   'o f f
s   u
t   'k i n d
d

Page 44
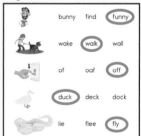

bunny	find	(funny)
wake	(walk)	wall
of	oaf	(off)
(duck)	deck	dock
lie	flee	(fly)

Page 45
1. with
2. kind
3. going
4. good

Page 46
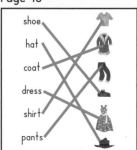

shoe
hat
coat
dress
shirt
pants

Answers

Page 47
1. coat 2. dress
3. shirt 4. hat
5. shoe 6. pants

Page 48
1. shirt 2. dress
3. pants

Page 49
1. pants 2. shoe
3. coat 4. hat

Page 50

show	(shoe)	shoo
(hat)	that	hut
cold	cot	(coat)
dry	(dress)	press
(shirt)	short	shut
ants	plants	(pants)

Page 51
Have someone check your answers.

Page 53
1. away 2. far
3. here 4. near

Page 54

Page 55
1. near 2. far
3. here 4. there
5. away

Page 57
1. him 2. again
3. may 4. by

Page 58

him	hum	(him)	hen	hem
them	(them)	thin	time	then
may	my	man	me	(may)
then	them	(then)	than	thin
by	buy	bee	(by)	be
again	gone	age	gain	(again)

Page 59
1. him 2. may
3. again 4. then
5. by

Page 60
1. him 2. then
3. again 4. by
5. them 6. may

Page 61

Page 62
1. then 2. there
3. pants 4. them

Page 63
1. dress 2. there
3. shirt 4. near

Page 65

Page 66

I eat bugs.
I live in a tree.
I show my teeth.
I hear with big ears.

Page 67

eat	(eat)	ate	at	ear
live	love	left	(live)	leave
show	snow	she	sow	(show)
hear	ear	(hear)	heart	hair
tell	tall	tile	(tell)	tale

Page 68
1. eat 2. live
3. tell 4. hear

Page 69
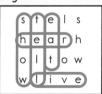

Page 70
Have someone check your answers.

Page 71
1. live 2. eat
3. show 4. tell
5. hear

Page 73
1. had 2. sat
3. ate 4. ran
5. found

Page 74

ran	run	rant	ram	(a)
did	dud	deed	(did)	dad
ate	(ate)	at	art	ant
sat	sit	(sat)	set	sad
had	head	hid	hat	(had)
found	round	fond	(found)	fund

Page 75
1. ran 2. found
3. sat 4. ate

Page 76
1. found 2. ate
3. ran 4. did
5. sat

Page 77
1. had 2. ate
3. ran

Page 78
1. present 2. party
3. from 4. thank
5. birthday 6. name

Page 79

Page 80
1. present 2. birthday
3. name 4. party

Page 81
1. False 2. True
3. True 4. False

Page 82
Have someone check your answers.

Page 83
1. name 2. party
3. thank 4. from

Page 84

Page 85
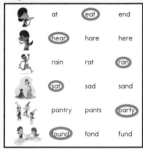

	at	(eat)	end
	(hear)	hare	here
	rain	rat	(ran)
	(sat)	sad	sand
	pantry	pants	(party)
	(found)	fond	fund

Page 86
1. had 2. party
3. ate 4. thank
5. present 6. shirt

Page 87
1. True 2. False
3. True 4. False

Page 89
1. soon 2. while
3. when 4. where
5. now

Page 90
1. now 2. when
3. while 4. where

Page 91

when	hen	wet	(when)	win
where	wear	were	here	(where)
now	(now)	new	no	mow
soon	son	(soon)	moon	sun
while	will	hill	(while)	wall

Page 93
1. any 2. well
3. stand 4. just
5. if 6. could

Page 94
1. well 2. stand
3. any 4. could

Page 95
1. well 2. stand
3. if 4. just

Answers

Page 96

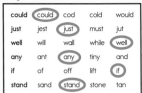

could	(could)	cod	cold	would
just	jest	(just)	must	jut
well	will	wall	while	(well)
any	ant	(any)	tiny	and
if	of	off	lift	(if)
stand	sand	(stand)	stone	tan

Page 97

1. well
2. could
3. just
4. stand
5. if
6. any

Page 98

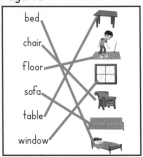

bed
chair
floor
sofa
table
window

Page 99

1. bed
2. window
3. sofa
4. floor
5. table
6. chair

Page 100

	bud	bet	(bed)
	(chair)	chore	hair
	four	(floor)	flour
	(sofa)	soft	soap
	able	(table)	tablet
	wind	meadow	(window)

Page 101

1. bed
2. chair
3. table
4. window

Page 102

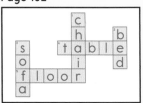

Page 103

1. True
2. False
3. True
4. True

Page 105

1. both
2. much
3. all
4. many
5. same
6. every

Page 106

1. both
2. every
3. all
4. some

Page 107

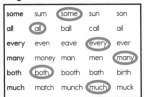

some	sum	(some)	sun	son
all	(all)	ball	call	ail
every	even	eave	(every)	ever
many	money	man	men	(many)
both	(both)	booth	bath	birth
much	match	munch	(much)	muck

Page 108

1. some
2. all
3. many
4. much

Page 109

1. every
2. both
3. much
4. many
5. all
6. some

Page 110

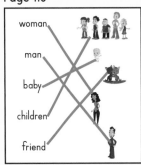

woman
man
baby
children
friend

Page 111

	worm	(woman)	woven
	men	map	(man)
	(baby)	bob	bubble
	chicken	child	(children)
	fried	(friend)	frond

Page 112

1. woman
2. friend
3. man
4. baby

Page 113

1. False
2. False
3. False
4. True

Page 114

1. woman
2. man
3. baby

Page 115

Have someone check
your answers.

Page 116

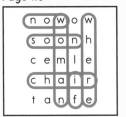

Page 117

1. tell
2. baby
3. all
4. now
5. present
6. duck
7. friend

Page 118

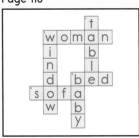

Page 119

1. soon
2. any
3. much
4. chair

Just a page per day with Sylvan workbooks helps kids catch up, keep up, and get ahead!

Review and Improve Skills • Grow Self-Confidence • Develop a Love of Learning!

Visit SylvanPagePerDay.com to find out more about doing a page per day of practice at home.